EPPING

TREED

Animal Life in the Trees

Green Tree Python

by Dee Phillips

Consultants:

Stephen Hammack
Terrestrial Ectotherm Keeper, Fort Worth Zoo, Fort Worth, Texas

Kimberly Brenneman, PhD
National Institute for Early Education Research, Rutgers University, New Brunswick, New Jersey

BEARPORT
PUBLISHING

New York, New York

Credits

Cover, © lunatic67/Shutterstock; 2–3, © fivespots/Shutterstock; 4, © Dirk Ercken/Shutterstock; 5, © Morris Mann/Shutterstock; 7, © apiguide/Shutterstock and © Joe McDonald/Science Photo Library; 8, © Eric Isselee/Shutterstock; 9, © Micha L. Reiser; 10–11, © Jean Paul Ferrero/Ardea; 12, © Neil Bowman/FLPA; 13, © fivespots/Shutterstock; 14, © Reinhold Leitner/Shutterstock; 15, © F. S. Westmorland/Science Photo Library; 16, © Gary Whitcombe; 17, © Carol Farneti-Foster/Getty Images; 18–19, © Janelle Lugge/Shutterstock and © Minden Pictures/Superstock; 20, © Snowleopard1/Istockphoto; 21, © Otto Plantema/Minden Pictures/FLPA; 22, © Matt Jeppson/Shutterstock, © Gerald A. DeBoer/Shutterstock, © Piotr Naskrecki/Minden Pictures/FLPA, © Sergey Uryadnikov/Shutterstock, © Luis M. Seco/Shutterstock, © Laila R/Shutterstock, © Jeffrey M. Frank/Shutterstock, and © Jason Patrick Ross/Shutterstock; 23TL, © lunatic67/Shutterstock; 23TC, © Carol Farneti-Foster/Getty Images; 23TR, © Neil Bowman/FLPA; 23BL, © Janelle Lugge/Shutterstock; 23BC, © mikeledray/Shutterstock; 23BR, © sean80II/Shutterstock; 24, © Matt Jeppson/Shutterstock, © Jason Patrick Ross/Shutterstock, © Gerry Ellis/Minden Pictures/FLPA, and © Wild Arctic Pictures/Shutterstock.

Publisher: Kenn Goin
Creative Director: Spencer Brinker
Editorial Director: Adam Siegel
Design: Emma Randall
Editor: Mark J. Sachner
Photo Researcher: Ruby Tuesday Books Ltd

Library of Congress Cataloging-in-Publication Data

Phillips, Dee, 1967–
  Green tree python / by Dee Phillips.
    p. cm. — (Treed: animal life in the trees)
  Includes bibliographical references and index.
  ISBN-13: 978-1-61772-909-6 (library binding)
  ISBN-10: 1-61772-909-4 (library binding)
 1. Green tree python—Juvenile literature. 2. Snakes—Juvenile literature. I. Title.
 QL666.O67P45 2014
 597.96'78—dc23

                    2013008327

For more information, write to Bearport Publishing Company, Inc., 45 West 21st Street, Suite 3B, New York, New York 10010. Printed in the United States of America.

10 9 8 7 6 5 4 3 2 1

Contents

Hanging Out 4

A Rain Forest Home 6

Long and Scaly 8

Life in the Trees 10

A Treetop Hunter 12

Time for Dinner 14

Snake Eggs 16

Baby Tree Pythons 18

Changing and Growing 20

Science Lab 22

Science Words 23

Index 24

Read More 24

Learn More Online 24

About the Author 24

Hanging Out

High up in a **rain forest** tree, a huge snake rests.

The animal is a green tree python.

Its long body is looped around a branch.

The snake is resting because it has just eaten a big meal.

It may not move or eat again for two weeks!

rain forest trees

green tree python

Adult green tree pythons spend their lives in trees. They sleep and hunt for food high above the ground.

A Rain Forest Home

Green tree pythons live in warm rain forests that are filled with trees.

The tall, leafy trees grow close together.

Green tree pythons make their homes among the tangled and twisted branches.

When the snakes get thirsty, they drink rainwater that has collected on a leaf.

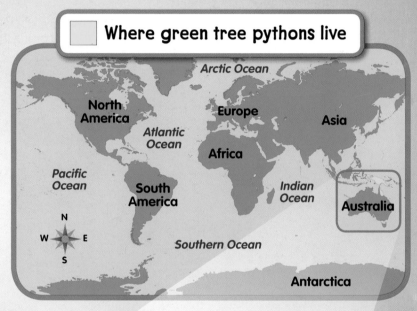

Where green tree pythons live

Look at the snake's body. What do you think it feels like?

There are many different types of pythons. Some live in rain forest trees. Others live in dry, rocky deserts or grasslands.

Long and Scaly

Like all snakes, pythons belong to a group of animals called **reptiles**.

All reptiles are **cold-blooded** and have scaly skin.

A green tree python's body is covered with **scales** that feel cool and dry.

The scales are little folds of tough skin that overlap each other.

Green tree pythons grow to about five feet (1.5 m) long. They live for around 15 to 19 years.

Measure a piece of string that is five feet (1.5 m) long. Lie down next to the string. Is a green tree python longer or shorter than you?

scales

Life in the Trees

Green tree pythons sleep during the day.

They might rest while hanging from a branch or curled up in a tree hole.

At night, pythons move around to hunt.

They look for a place where a meal might pass by.

The snakes slowly move from branch to branch until they find just the right spot.

To move along a branch, a green tree python uses special scales on its belly. The scales grip the branch and push the snake's body forward.

A Treetop Hunter

Once a snake has found a good place to hunt, it gets ready to attack.

It wraps its tail tightly around a branch.

The front part of its body hangs in the air in an S shape.

When a small animal, such as a rat, scurries along a branch, the snake strikes!

rat

Green tree pythons eat small animals that live in trees, such as rats, lizards, birds, and frogs.

S shape

Time for Dinner

A green tree python grabs its **prey** with its mouth.

At the same time, its tail tightly holds on to the branch.

Then the python wraps its long body around the unlucky creature.

The snake squeezes so hard that the animal can't breathe and dies.

Finally, the snake swallows its prey whole—head first!

A green tree python can open its mouth wide enough so that an animal that's bigger than the snake's head can fit inside.

15

Snake Eggs

Adult green tree pythons live alone, but they come together to **mate**.

About 75 days later, a female snake lays up to 30 eggs in a hole in a tree.

The baby snakes inside the eggs need to stay warm to grow.

So the mother snake wraps her body around the eggs.

After about 50 days, baby pythons hatch from the eggs.

Unlike a chicken egg, a snake egg doesn't have a hard shell. Instead, its shell feels like soft leather.

mother green
tree python

baby green
tree python

egg

Describe the baby pythons
in the picture. How are they
similar to and different
from their mother?

Baby Tree Pythons

The newly hatched pythons are 12 inches (30 cm) long.

Unlike their parents, they aren't green.

Instead, some are yellow, while others are dark red.

Once they hatch, the little pythons can take care of themselves.

They climb out of the tree hole and start hunting.

baby green tree pythons

Baby green tree pythons spend a lot of their time in tree branches close to the ground. They live in open areas of the forest where there are fewer trees.

How do you think the colors of baby tree pythons help them?

Changing and Growing

Many animals hunt baby pythons.

Luckily, the snakes' colors help them blend in with branches that are close to the ground.

After about six months, the baby pythons' scales turn green.

Now they can safely live high in the trees.

Their green color helps them hide from enemies in the leafy branches.

In two to three years, the pythons will mate and have babies of their own.

a young green tree python eating a frog

Many animals, including large lizards and snakes, eat baby green tree pythons. Birds, such as owls, hawks, and eagles, hunt for young and adult green tree pythons.

21

Science Lab

Animal Hide-and-Seek

Fur or skin that helps an animal blend into the place where it lives is called camouflage. A green tree python's color helps it hide among leafy trees in the rain forest.

Look at the four animals and four habitats pictured below. Then match each animal to the habitat where it blends in the best.

| thorny lizard | leopard frog | katydid | polar bear |

| rain forest | tundra | desert | pond |

How does camouflage help protect animals?
How do you think camouflage helps some animals catch food?

(The answers are on page 24.)

Science Words

cold-blooded (KOHLD-*bluhd*-id) having a body temperature that goes up or down to match the temperature of the air or water around one's body

mate (MAYT) to come together to produce young

prey (PRAY) animals hunted by other animals

rain forest (RAYN FOR-ist) a place where many trees and other plants grow, and lots of rain falls

reptiles (REP-tilez) cold-blooded animals, such as snakes and lizards, that have dry, scaly skin, a backbone, and lungs for breathing

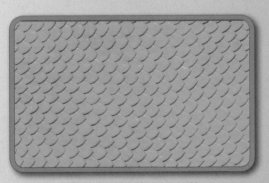

scales (SKAYLZ) small pieces of hard skin that cover the body of a snake or other reptile

Index

babies 16–17, 18–19, 20–21
cold-blooded 8
drinking 6
eggs 16–17
enemies 20–21
food 4–5, 10, 12–13, 14–15, 20

hunting 5, 10, 12, 14–15, 18
length 8, 18
life span 8
mating 16, 20
mother snakes 16–17
mouth 14

rain forests 4, 6–7
reptiles 8
scales 8–9, 11, 20
skin colors 18, 20
sleeping 4–5, 10

Read More

Clark, Willow. *Green Tree Pythons.* New York: Rosen (2012).

Fiedler, Julie. *Pythons.* New York: Rosen (2008).

McCarthy, Cecilia. *Green Tree Pythons.* Mankato, MN: Capstone (2012).

Learn More Online

To learn more about green tree pythons, visit **www.bearportpublishing.com/Treed**

About the Author

Dee Phillips lives near the ocean on the southwest coast of England. She develops and writes nonfiction and fiction books for children of all ages.

Answers for Page 22

A thorny lizard lives in the desert.

A leopard frog lives near a pond.

A katydid lives in a rain forest.

A polar bear lives on the tundra.

Camouflage helps animals stay hidden from enemies that want to eat them. For example, the katydid and leopard frog hide from birds. Camouflage also helps some animals hide from their prey. For example, a polar bear blends in with the snow and ice when it's hunting seals.